# INSIDE OUT

poems by

Chrys Salt

Autolycus Press
London

*To Richard, for all his love and support,*
*and for my family.*

*My thanks to Hubert Nicholson for 25 years of friendship and encouragement.*



This book was set using Palatino 11 point on the University of London Phototypesetter.


Autolycus Press,
14 Barlby Road, London W10 6AR

ISBN 0 903413 43 4

# Contents

## *Old promises. . . . .*



## *Inside out. . . . .*

## *Writing these poems*

When all the words are congregated
and say 'yes'
and the metronome tocks
to a beat I recognise
and the orchestra, tuned and ready to play
for countless angels poised upon a pin,
scrapes no chair and focuses
on the moment to begin,
in she will burst through the double doors,
say, 'Here I am!',
and here she is indeed.
So predictable.
So inevitable.
So precisely as I would have expected.

# *Old promises*

## *Old promises*

I have grown out of my old promises,
but these I make to you fit snug, like skin.
Not asking you to believe the old adages;
love is not forever. Nor would I win
your heart by minimising the old allegiances,
for such deceptions wear a little thin.
Asking you simply to investigate new mysteries
with me, promising a little boat to travel in
(a short journey on not always tranquil seas).
I have grown out of my old promises
and now wear only these.

## *Daffodils at Christmas*

Gay as a blackbird's beak
your daffodils unbud
and burst into frilled trumpets
this Christmas morning,
bringing a torch of freshness
to the season's ritual;
reminding the heart's cold bulb
of its green forgotten centre.
Better to have left the corner bare
than focus this bright beam
on the chill comfort I have grown to.
Better not to dare
this incandescent flame
for fear its clear and unexpected shining
blinds me into love,
and, sweeter than sap, your gentleness
enters my bones,
calling my roots to draw up joy again.

# *Mitcham Green*

The tree was singing.
Winter branches leaved with singing birds,
jostling in chirruping congregations,
flexing the twig-tips
or flung like blown paper-scraps
against the pidgeon-grey breast
of the evening. Dense on the boughs
as summer foliage;
fluttering, shaken (as summer leaves are shaken)
and singing!
Such a hullabaloo, such a carolling of sparrows.

How beautiful it was,
this jubilation,
this hallelujah of bird-song!
as the traffic growled round the green
headlight to tail-light
and the chill urban dusk deepened
and the homing shoppers
shoved and jabbered
as if they had not heard.

Oh, it seemed to me
that only the tree
with its birds mattered.
And all things else, absurd.

# *Tiger, tiger. . . .*

Ride this tiger with me,
this dangerous, impossible, possible beast,
running amok, firing our lives
suddenly, with his fierce, bright, stripes.
He is wild this one,
stopping only from time to time for passengers.
On the rampage
he will carry us beyond reason,
into his jungle country, hot and insular
(each feather on each bird
drawn with a sharp pencil;
trees, burnt into the sky,
fruit on the farthest branches visible).
Come while the flame is in the tiger's eye
a leap beyond these line we've settled in,
for soon enough that roar
which severs sleep from will
and sets each sparkling hair upright
will dwindle like a candle-end:
touch that bolts lightning will earth
in quiet talk; our tiger skinned
and wrapped about us like an old man's rug,
the embers dimming in his eyes of glass.

# *Where to now, love? (I)*

Where to now, love?
No way back.
No more signposts
on a beaten track.
No more knowing
what tomorrow holds
(castle or dragon)
as the way unfolds.
Sitting close together,
trembling to be near,
bodies touch through fabric
everything unclear.
Holding to the minute
like a drowning man
shall we when the journey's done
know where we began?
Mortgages and washing;
mother round for tea.
What would in the end, love
be left of you and me?

# *Dove*

I tell you, only with honour I became
a small dove cradled in your palm.
With breeder's skill you gentled me;
took from the dove-cote one whitened with ease,
safe from the dangerous talons of regret.
Proud, because then you thought me beautiful;
glad, for you scanned my landscape
and made peace with me. We need nothing
to reaffirm us in this recognition
because you were clothed in humility
and I, with the dove's innocence, trusted
myself to all the terrors of your hand.

# *The morning it snowed*

Wellingtons gleamed like jet in the hall
on the morning it snowed
(the children running from window to window)
and I brought you tea, as the silence
drifted against the walls
of the house under the cold pearl of the morning.
Surprising how the garden could change overnight
into something otherwise;
confections of sugar, skeins of flung lace,
all the familiar contours masked and blurred,
thistle and rose bush gloved in a white strangeness,
birdbath and barrow filled and furred
and some things wholly lost
under that unexpected snowfall.

On the morning it snowed
(sitting together
across the cereal bowls, the empty cups –
our landscape changed utterly since nightfall
and this altered map)
I watched you push your toastcrumbs into a heap
with your forefinger
and cradled your foot, like a cat, in my lap.

## *For the first day of spring*

'Not baroque', you said, 'rococo'.
But anyway Tartini.
And outside the window
the sticky buds thrusting –
and our thighs were sticky
with one another,
and our thrusting
was for the same reason –
to taste the sun
and open all the windows of the heart
to let in spring!

## *Daffodils*

I cannot look at daffodils without
remembering.
A blunt gesture on a wet afternoon.
The yellow trumpets
shouting that you loved me.
The sticky juice seeping
onto my hand
through the wet tissue.
The rain on the petals.
And you in the room
waiting to be touched.

# *Waking at dawn*

Half awake, I feel your smooth hand move
between the sheets. Not as a hawk
swoops on a dove, not to prove
mastery – but with intimacy, like talk
in a private room. Your possession
of all I am is gentler than passion.

And I, submissive in my sleep, turn
like a dolphin on your wave
and, mesmerised by touch, learn
dawn in braille. Am what I have,
become what you possess,
and open like a flower to consciousness.

# *Exhibit*

Water, in a cut-glass tumbler
on the window ledge, in the sun.
So it was.
And so in simple images the heart invests.
(Beneath the sheet our following curves
describe each other.
                    Words,
less than the sum of all their parts,
confuse.)
A spar of light fires many-sided prisms.
Listen: the full carillon of a single bird.

# *Jingle*

(for my children)

I love you more than upwards
And further down than down
And if the circle's wide enough
I love you round and round.

And more than liquorice allsorts
And deeper than the sky
I love the you inside of you
More questioning than why.

I love you more than upwards
And further down than down
And if the circle's wide enough
I love you round and round.

With love that's sweet as reason–
More positive than yes
And safer than the turtle
Inside her carapace.

I love you more than upwards
And further down than down
And if the circle's wide enough
I love you round and round.

# *Yes poem*

If it be yes
it must be yes
that is
and speaks with tongues,
the bright yes
of the soul,
the bottomless
unmuddied, clear
true yes
of certain always
doubts put by.
The yes that asks
no questions,
tells no lie,
each lesser yes
is but a shade
of no.
Yes is
and will
and when yes speaks
we know!

# *A winter's tale*

Loving together
is all I can offer you
(parting be kind to you,
give you fair weather).
This is our winter
(firelight and candlelight),
joy in my eyes tonight
bright as a splinter.
Under the counterpane,
nestle like children
(desperate in lover's lane
ranges a dragon).
Morning be marvellous,
rouse at our waking
one more brave day for us
better for laughing.
Wearing the days between
now and tomorrow,
love will grow elbow-thin
(letting in sorrow).
Loving together
is all I can offer you
(loving be glad for you,
give you fair weather).

# *Infidelity (I)*

Although, my darling, absence makes the heart
less fond, and distances that part
hands settle the sense again
into accustomed gestures.
                    Although to sustain
love when the heart is comfortable
(eating and drinking at a familiar table)
is an impossible task (for what we *dare*
is not to be confused with what we *are*;
and what we say, merely an assonance
designed to rhyme obliquely with our sense).
Yet, dear, of you I ask the impossible
(to hunt a haystack for the preposterous needle),
knowing the merciful daily ritual
obscures the pulsing of the wanton will,
and there are distances we may not cross,
sustaining nothing but a sense of loss.

# *Kites (I)*

Striving against spring gusts
we watched the kites
pull on invisible strings,
swerving, redoubling against the light.
Some flown to specks
and others close and still
like technicoloured patches
on the sky,
and some whose will
seemed to defy
their landlocked handlers
as they danced
in dives and snatches
flirting with the air.

There is something magical and true
in grown men flying kites,
and on that afternoon it seemed
they all would stay
forever caught in hammocks of the wind,
their bright tails streaming.
And marvelling with the children
(yours and mine)
I felt your nearness tug
as my thoughts went flying
free, but responsive to an unseen line.

# *Kites (II)*

Keep to my line, so I can fly
Lest I go floundering round the sky,
The victim of my randomness.
Possess, so I can dispossess.

Keep to my line and centre me.
Own me, my own, so setting free
My wildness and my wantonness,
Custodian of my release.

Keep to my line that, rash but true,
My point of reference be you
And when a keen wind fells my flight
Be proof to me against its bite.

Keep to my line, though absence, time,
Distance divide. Keep to my line
This powerful paradox to show –
Hold me, so you can let me go.

# *Mending fences*

Beneath the fallen fence
the flower-bed suffocates,
has nowhere to grow.

We will mend fences tomorrow, you say.

But though the barriers are down
fierce territorial imperatives
forestall our stampede
into the neighbouring garden.
An urban Gandhi
breeding curry leaves
under his tea-roses
mildly attempts the gap
with the universal language of grins.

Without the fence
the children, who do not observe
such niceties,
rampage over his borders
delighted
and mend fences today.

# *Lost childhood*

On the fruitdrop-green grass
minted with daisies
a liquorice bird
pulled a bubblegum worm
sucked to a point
on a candyfloss skyline
icelolly lupins
in chocolate loam
humbugged with bees
the marzipan shadows
of alyssum heaped
with marshmallow pinks
gobstopper sunlight
on smartie-bright Leggo
lollipop childhood
dropped on the lawn.

# *Roses and vipers*

Make the ordinary, extraordinary
by thinking better of it.
Catch sonnets in teacups!
Cherish the commonplace
(for that is most of it).
Suck love from the reluctant lips
of domesticity
(that takes so much of it)
and make your thumbnail of the tapestry
intricate with possibility
before you've done with it.
Risk all. Only in covertness
lie wounds and hazards,
for at the end of it
each one of us carries
between umbilicus and grave
her private basket of roses and vipers.
And that is all of it.
We shall not live
(or not the best of it)
unless we dare
(chancing our arm deep down in it)
beauty and dangers.

# *Breakfast*

In the kitchen the shape you make
catches my attention.
You move softly; stone tiles, bare feet;
re-organising objects that are not wholly familiar;
making my coffee almost as I like it;
moving, without agitation, as spring
knocks for the windows to be opened.

I ask if this is what I wanted,
while you make space in the kitchen.

The children squabble over the Marmite
or a knife.
I shriek from my bubble.
Their selfish little faces crumple.
There is no room in me to be sorry.
They are unmaking me!

Where is serene motherhood this morning?
She of the composed countenance?
My monster screams, 'It is enough!
I will drown you,
drown all of you in Branflakes!'

You do not escape my attention
as you drape the clothes-horse with washing,
for today, at least, you walk with me
on my nails of misery and rage.

It is enough.

# *Welsh incident*

In a gateway at the threshold of my valley
the wind-combed grass, darkened
with shadows of homing birds;
the arc of a small field falling away
and broken by standing nettles,
we stood, wearing the silence together
and holding our breath with Wales.
Some mist or vapour told us
where the Conwy slept
and where the sea, invisible and vast,
shimmered like foil behind the mountain wall;
the sun marking its exit with a stain of peach;
tomorrow's weather, brewing in a boiling cloud-mass.

That landscape now has entered me forever,
for I will never again
stand at that field's end
with someone I love as much as you,
certain that, whatever comes after,
this much is true.

# *Owl*

Down soundless avenues of dusk
she swerves; hangs like a mobile
on an unseen string, piercing the jungle hedgerow
with her eye.

The still air, redolent with musk of rose and badger,
        waits:
and she sustains her predatory tension
like a single deadly dancer, poised
kite-high against day's ebbing haze of blue.

Under the vivid dandelion
trembles the red-toothed shrew.

# *The basilisk*

Wary of weasels. Stuffing his ears
with serpent fingers at cockcrow. Avoiding mirrors –
his fatal three – the toad-hatched basilisk
stalks stones across his selfmade wilderness.
His toxic breath blasts flower to fossil, his
glance spawns desert dust beneath the moon's thin
        disc.
Only the weasel is fearless
and will enter a death struggle on the blackened
        grass.

When dead the basilisk is terrible
no longer, but nailed to household doors
like warning moles, frights merely spiders–
a hieroglyph of former terrors,
and safe at last from cockcrow or weasel
or his own deadly image in a glass.

# *A country walk with the children in October*

A hillside, sheep-mown,
a swollen bellyful of root
and seed and stone.
Yes – velvet.
Reluctant chaperones,
we bribe, cajole, threaten to shoot
daughters and sons
to share it.
Divesting summer's loan
the costumed wood of leaf and fruit
strips to the bone,
winds shake it.
The offspring drag and moan
and climb and claim another sweet
at each milestone,
don't see it.
A cart-track overgrown,
crunching with acorns underfoot,
a forest sewn –
a blanket
of beachnut, fir and cone.
The polished blackberry to loot,
wild and fullblown
we pluck it.
A makeshift xylophone –
a branch against a farmyard gate –
rattles a tune
imperfect.

Touch, sight, smell all ingrown
they clamour at the choice of route
in whining tone.
We wear it.
Tractors and children drone.
Our mute wish, as we stride on resolute,
to be alone
and own it.

## *The chameleon*

Why do you come to me in these colours?
The colours of your dark self?
They are on your hands, in the corners
of the room; they brush off on me
like dust from the wings of moths.
Why do you wear 'no' like a badge
when we have dressed in 'yes' so often;
when we have walked the cliff pathways
robed in green wind,
tacked about us with birdflight?
Or worn nothing together but the
pastel and silk of skin?
Like the chameleon I draw your hue;
am lost on this grey branch you offer.
Why do you come to me in these colours?
The colours of this dark you?

# *Fishing*

Mouth-roof cleft on a barbed hook,
dragging water in a following swift vee
and landward lurching,
death seems certain.
Then, suddenly slack,
the taut line drops a curve
and darting back
to weed-furred, pebble-cobbled ocean floor
to hide, salve wounds, regenerate,
be as before
in some dim, unremitting haunt of home.
But no!
the barbed hook bites.
Again, blood, bubbles, flurried mud.
Sunlight, like fists of crystal flung,
and death seems preferable.
The just line joining us
hauls me back in.

# *Testing the drop*

How close you were
hanging over the abyss by your finger-ends.
One stamp on their straining tips
you would have fallen
as deep as pride is.
A breeze would have taken you
and you would still be falling.

(About their stalks, the leaves of the yellow
chrysanthemums
had withered like an omen,
the pane condensed to tears.)

Spurning my hand, you tested the drop,
feet dangling. Oh Christ
will it always be one or other of us
hanging there; tempting danger to its last ditch;
always just making the ledge
before the rock breaks loose
or the turf frays from our grasp
under the safe shelf?

(High on their stems, the chrysanthemums
blazed like noon;
the window refracting rainbow.)

By doing nothing I could let you fall,
but with a gesture
I retrieve myself!

# *Fossil*

This stone I hold,
this imprint of a shell
we found on Sussex slopes
when all was well.

Content that day
to laze where orchids lank
littered the furzy face
of a white bank.

How pleased you were
to find the fossil
where the coast was so remote
from that chalk spur.

A petrified
relic of history
which swam where harebells grow
that once was sea.

One of all things.
One trace of an outdone
ecology. One day
looked back upon.

And such as shell's
impression in the stone,
a day that's etched in me,
once live, now gone.

# *In service*

Because your loving is so good
And I cannot repay
One kindness more than any could
Nor dare to hear you pray.

Because I cast you as a clown
And made you sing your song
When all your tears were tumbling down
And all the words were wrong.

Because my care can only be
Inside the limits of a kiss,
Forgive the silly heart of me
That cannot love you as you wish.

You make me queen again, and serve
My least commandment with your blood.
Don't love me more than I deserve,
Or any more than any should.

# *Infidelity (II)*

Again the snow comes.
This time between us;
covering tracks, making the roads impassable.
I think of you,
reading a paper in your usual chair
or slicing snow from your footway
and measure distance in snowflakes
endlessly falling.
Defecting to domesticity, the limbs forget
sense ringing to its marrow,
nights worn thin with talk.
Past alien frontiers,
you are where no long touch may reach
or dreams may cross.
Where (inaccessible to care) a stranger walks
with creaturehood whose customs, speech
I cannot know.
(More than the snow divides us
each from each.)
And though the heart pulls hard,
the old ways fasten us,
familiarity engulfs us like a shroud.

## *Morning sickness*

I wake to grief that nothing shakes
and there is nothing in the whole bleak world
that makes good reason to be glad
without your body's bloom against my face.

I wake to fear, and reason dislocates.
Cure me with trust. My sickness breeds
imaginings of other travellers on your land
making discovery of my secret place.

I wake to pain with love's sharp nail
grown inward. Each tensing fibre waits
for confirmation of despair. Come home
with flowers dear love and eyes with truth in them.

Cure me with care.

# *My love has found a new mirror*

My love has found a new mirror to reflect him.
Making a fresh attempt at himself
he becomes what he sees in it.
The old glass lies, shows
whom he would not know.
Fairest of all to me he is in it.

My love grows big to a new hand that livens him.
He walks the greener grass of himself
on a day without history in it.
And though the old days clamour behind him
the mirror blinds him,
his first impression dancing so bright in it.

My beloved disowns my loved likeness of him
wanting no more to see himself
wanting no more of it,
and I grieve and I grieve and I roar
like a dog at the door
repeating, repeating, repeating my mindless belief in it.

# *Parting*

Not knowing if we will ever again
touch in the old way;
or whether we will touch at all.
Not knowing if I will come again
to this room and stay
until the bones ring and the night grows tall.

Not showing (even a chink) that I care
much in the old way.
Not showing that I care at all
(no longer on my sleeve) I will wear
wanting, turned away
with its face to the bricks in the wall.

And moving apart, perhaps the sense will harden,
snatch at the old way
only when caught unaware.
Leaping like seaspray less and less often
at steps on the pathway;
a clamour of keys, or gloves on a chair.

## *Where to now, love? (II)*

Where to now, love,
Anywhere?
Mind over mattering
careless of care.
Bird in the hand, love,
bleeding in your palm
what will come of harm, love?
Nothing, love, but harm.
Castles in the air, love,
make nowhere to hide.
Tiger at the gate still
waits for you to ride.
I would build a bridge, love,
you would make a dam.
You are what you are, love.
I am what I am.
Everything uncertain
but this much is true!
I will go on loving.
What will become of you?

# *Lament*

A girl comes to your gate
with flowers
in a sweet wind;
in a thin dress.
(You cannot stop,
you are late for a business appointment.)
You take the flowers.
Yes!
She lingers, though the year
darkens
and grow colder
and is sunless
(the petals drop).
To her it's
of no matter, resigning
herself to waiting.
Yes,
and when you come to her
no flowers
but her still hands
on her thin dress
(this time you stop)
folded like
two long cold white lily-buds.
You touch her fingers.
Yes.

## *Speedwell*

I washed your sheets today
(our love-stains purged)
and watched them billowing
like spinnakers of boats
on a green bay.
The lawn was choppy
but the March sky
the colour of speedwell.
And thought of the journey
we had made
in a cockle-shell
of poems, such as this;
reckless on winter tides
that ebbed and surged
(no fair wind following)
and of your going away.

## *After Eden*

Entering his room
she brought delight
like a basket of apples.

Now she has no cause.

*Inside out*

# *Inside out*

My poems wear me Inside Out,
My fraying seams, my knotted wool,
My hanging threads too visible
Of guilt and pain, of hate and sin.
No sense of place.
No social grace.
My poems wear me Outside In.

# *Not preferred*

Filching slices of meat
like silver-fish in grease
from the Sunday platter
got up my mother's nose.
Enraged her, so
her two-pronged fork
would have kebabed my hand.
Into my brother
she pushed succulent slices,
seeking his heart with meat-juice,
stuffing his face with mother-love.
I was too fat. Too greedy.
When had my fingers last seen soap?
I was too. . . . . everything.
How would she cope!

Over the kitchen cabinet's
enamelled flap
my grubby scavenger
met his rosy princeling,
watched her carve.
He was in her good books.
I was under her feet,
perplexed, uncertain always
how I'd erred.

She never wiped my mouth with her pinny
though I would have done anything. . .
even become a vegetarian.

## *Mummy, I can't get past you*

Mummy, I can't get past you.
You stand in my way
until I outlast you,
and nothing I say
will ever unmask you.

Mummy, why don't I know you?
The size of that child
you whittle me down to
still unreconciled
to not having found you.

Mummy, why can't I love you?
I want you to love,
to hold you, to have you.
So what must I prove?
Will none of me move you?

## *Leavetaking*

Frederick Arthur Salt 1907 - 1971

I washed my hands in a little water,
I dressed in a dark colour
and walked in grief behind my mother
through the September sunlight
to the funeral car.
        Under
the ginger chrysanthemums
the suffocating pastel carnations
was the coffin
where they had put my father.
I knew his head and shoulders
were at the wide end of the box
under the flowers
and his feet, with their long toes, tapered
where the coffin narrowed.
I imagined that his arms were crossed.
I imagined him dressed in white garments
arranged in ordered folds;
my gentle father
lying like a stone knight
under the nailed lid.

I came too late to see you, daddy,
I missed you beached in that bleached hospital.
Nor knew, until too late,
that the last time
was the last time.

How long must I dog your box of bones
down those orphaned streets,
a neighbour in every mourning gateway,
under that same September sky?
When can I cast you off
like a Viking pyre
into the warm darkness of my remembering
and the perfumed air,
finish the journey with you
and consign you, at loving last,
        to the fire?

Daddy, I want to say goodbye.

# *Therapy*

Margaret, Margaret,
drop your bucket in my well,
ding dong bell.

The bucket falls five fathoms down,
down with a hollow empty sound.
Ding dong
ding dong bell.

I  bring the landscape of my week into your room,
'the pain, the calm and the astonishment',
you are impassive in your orange chair
the Pythoness on the tripod dressed as mummy.
You and the room and the place I sit
and the vase with all its pearly colours
and the picture with the cracked corner
and the pastel urn on your wall,
and sometimes daffodils, are a place of safety
that waits for me at the week's end.

The bucket falls five fathoms down,
down with a hollow empty sound.
Down for sorrow, down for gold,
down for a secret never to be told.
Ding dong
ding dong bell.

I have left undone those things I ought to have done
and done those things I ought not to have done.
Who will have mercy on me?

An immutable world like a scene
in a bauble.
        My entering flurries the leaves;
tinkles the glass,
shakes the petals of the daffodils
but alters nothing here.
Hurricane, holocaust,
coup and counter-coup,
have no relevance.
This place has a fine focus
on the very centre of the soul.

The bucket falls five fathoms down,
down with a hollow empty sound.
Down for sorrow, down for gold,
down for a secret never to be told.
Nothing of him that doth change. . .
Ding dong
ding dong bell.

Margaret, Margaret,
Love me. Love me not.
Judge me. Judge me not.
Help me, forgive me.
Ding dong bell.

# *Carol in Juniors*

Tasselled with ringlets
Was Carol in Juniors.
Bum big as Birmingham
Face like a gibbon.
Carol in Juniors
Pinned up and parcelled
With butterfly hairslides
And satiny ribbon.
Puckered and dimpled
All over with smocking.
Socks that were star-bright,
Socks never dropping.
Me in my hand-me-down
Liberty bodice.
Jumpers refurbished
From several-hand wool.
God, how I hated her,
Carol in Juniors!
Carol whose mum
Always came up to school.

# *Graffiti artist*

Zed is dead
but lives on walls of lavatories
on garage doors
and sides of trains.

His mother said,
'Don't play on sidings , Zed,
please use your brains'.
But Zed and Chic and Spam
just did two fingers
with their spray-can hand.

Now Zed is dead
ripped by a fast train
from a tunnel wall
while mother thought him
still at school.
He used his brains
to spray his final say:
'Zed Rules. O.K.?'

# *Punk*

'I love you, mum' with bleeding heart
his biceps' legend ran.
How could she love what he'd become
who'd held him unengraved
in babyhood; that pastel ungraffitied
with this occult bestiary
of dragon, bird and crucifix?
Not how she'd pictured him
this egghead cockatoo
tattooed from brow to chin
with hideous webs;
all her proud hopes
that he would play the violin
read books and have a bank account
crossed out and scribbled on.
Her eye's apple fallen
with a gravity beyond reason.

Was there a crossword clue
amongst the swastikas, the doves
and skulls, the titsy ladies
and the clambering spiders,
the leather, chains and safety pins?
The double message inked across his fingers?

## *A child without a face meets Princess Di*

A child without a face
meets Princess Di.
Nothing of beauty
but her rain-bright eyes
in Dulux corridors.
Dark
deep-lashed
big poppy centres
bobbing a grateful curtsy
in a noseless
bomb-rased landscape
that no longer blooms.

# *Stephen: in care*

Stephen smells terrible,
at seventeen
he doesn't know where mashed potatoes start.
Stephen
thinks dinner is always eaten
to a percussion of cutlery,
that beds come in rows
and are always dressed the same.
Stephen craps with the door ajar
as a safety precaution
and wipes his bum on paper that crackles.
When Stephen grew hairy
he thought he was going ape
and hid for days without an explanation.
For Stephen
Mum and Dad are what other people have.
For Stephen
cuddles are strictly professional.
For Stephen
the cabbage has been too long
on the boil.

# *Bomb-blast*

Yesterday it rained broken
people
who could not be mended.

It rained exploded luggage
tickets and
student plimsolls,
disposable
forks and knives,
hostesses, wedding rings, presents for Christmas
that would not be given.

It rained half finished
sentences
gestures and games
and plans
and wives,
chocolates
and
soaps
and seatbelts,
miniature gins,
safety harnesses,
comics
and little children
who would not arrive.

Yesterday it rained broken people,
falling and ended.
And words don't come out right.
The American envoy's face is grey and tight:
'What kind of man could do such things. . .
The nation mourns. . . defies belief. . .'
Quotable clichés for the tabloid press
chasing themselves around his grief,
around our own.
The far-flung dead are marked
with makeshift flags
and temporary shrouds of plastic bags.

# *It landed on my page and I killed it with 'The Penguin Book of Contemporary British Poetry'*

A fly, no bigger than a crumb,
no match for me.
The very worst it could have done
was make me itch, but then it seemed
to me to make the room unclean.
And that is why it had to die.
Now on my empty page it lies.
Such little deaths epitomise
the cruel and senseless things we do.

I am sorry, little fly,
I wasn't thinking about you!

# *Big for my boots*

If you would enter, knock and ask for Chrys,
I am in here, but nothing as I seem;
For I am *me*, big, bold and glad,
Not small and painted-on like this.
The face I wear is my disguise,
I watch you through the peepholes of my eyes.
My skin, my dress, wrinkle and hem
Give shape and matter to the Chrys I am
And tight they feel so great I grow,
I'm splitting out through blouse and shoe
And pushing things from desk and shelf.
I just cannot contain myself !